THE EMOTION COMPASS

Navigating Your Feelings to Find Balance

KEISHA MCDONALD, LPC

1st edition book Design: Keisha McDonald
Production: AmourLegaci Publishing
Editing: Keisha McDonald
Publisher: AmourLegaci Publishing
To order: Amazon.com
Author Website: AmourLegaci.com
Printed in the United States of America

MADD Therapy Counseling and Coaching: MADDTherapy.com

A note from the author

Are you someone who likes to self help? Maybe you just don.t like dealing with people at this time in your life or ever! Well, this workbook will help you help yourself with changing how your emotions affect you.

Obviously , if this doesn.t work you will need to pull out the big compass...

Your phone, and call a therapist!

Happy Navigating!

Keisha McDonald, LPC

Daily Quote

YOU GOT THIS!

KEEP BELIEVING IN YOURSELF

EMBRACE THE JOURNEY, TRUST YOUR ABILITIES.

Unlock the doors of possibility with the key of self-belief. Embrace your inner strength and trust in your abilities to conquer any challenges that may come your way. With self-belief as your guiding light, you have the power to unlock doors that lead to growth, success, and fulfillment. Believe in yourself, for you hold the key to a future filled with endless possibilities.

EVERY STEP FORWARD IS A VICTORY, TRUST THE PROCESS.

Your journey is special, and every challenge helps you grow. Trust that as your journey continues, it can change your life. Be brave, keep going, and find amazing things in the everyday steps of your journey. Embrace each moment with an open heart and a curious mind. Every tiny step you take forward is progress on your journey to success.

Trust the process and celebrate small victories that pave the way to your dreams. You've got the strength to turn aspirations into reality; your journey is a canvas awaiting your unique brushstroke. Embrace the adventure, face uncertainties with a fearless heart, and remember: You got this! Believe in the incredible potential within you, and watch your story unfold into a masterpiece of success and self-discovery.

YOU GOT THIS! ✳ YOU GOT THIS! ✳ YOU GOT THIS!

Welcome to The Emotion Compass!

This is a guide offering practical tools, empowering techniques Unlocking Self-Awareness for Emotional Wellness

In these pages, you'll embark on a journey of self-discovery and emotional awareness. This book is your companion in understanding and navigating the vast landscape of your emotions, guiding you towards greater self-awareness and emotional well-being.

Throughout this journey, you will learn to recognize and acknowledge your emotions with clarity and compassion. By delving into the depths of your inner world, you'll uncover patterns and insights that empower you to respond to life's challenges with resilience and authenticity.

Here, you'll find practical tools and exercises designed to help you process and manage your emotions effectively. Whether you're exploring joy, navigating sadness, embracing peace, or confronting anxiety, each page offers guidance to cultivate emotional intelligence and foster personal growth.

Emotional well-being is not just about feeling good—it's about understanding yourself deeply, responding to life's ups and downs with grace, and nurturing a balanced inner harmony. This book is your ally in cultivating a richer, more fulfilling life through the power of emotional awareness and self-discovery.

Get ready to embark on a transformative journey. Embrace the wisdom within these pages, and empower yourself to live more fully, authentically, and joyfully.

Welcome to the beginning of your emotional wellness journey.

An "emotion compass" is a metaphorical tool or concept used to help individuals navigate their emotional landscape. Just as a physical compass helps you find your direction in the physical world, an emotion compass assists in understanding and managing your emotions, guiding you toward emotional balance and well-being. Here.s a deeper look at what an emotion compass entails:

Key Concepts of an Emotion Compass

Emotional Awareness:
- Identifying Emotions: Recognizing and naming your emotions accurately. Knowing what you are feeling is the first step toward managing those feelings effectively.
- Understanding Triggers: Being aware of what triggers certain emotions in you, whether they are external events, thoughts, or physical states.

Emotional Regulation:
- Managing Intensity: Learning techniques to manage the intensity of your emotions so they do not overwhelm you.
- Coping Strategies: Developing healthy coping mechanisms to deal with difficult emotions, such as deep breathing, mindfulness, or talking to a friend.

Direction and Purpose:
- Guiding Actions: Using your emotions as a guide to make decisions that align with your values and goals. For instance, feelings of discomfort might signal that something needs to change.
- Emotional Goals: Setting emotional goals, such as achieving a state of calm, happiness, or confidence, and using the compass to navigate toward these states.

Practical Applications of an Emotion Compass

Daily Check-ins:
- Self-Reflection: Regularly take a few moments to reflect on your emotional state. Ask yourself what you are feeling and why.
- Journaling: Keep a journal to track your emotions and identify patterns over time. This can help in understanding how your emotions influence your behavior and decisions.

Emotional Mapping:
- Emotion Wheel: Use an emotion wheel, a tool that categorizes emotions to help you pinpoint exactly what you are feeling. This can enhance your emotional vocabulary and awareness.
- Mind Mapping: Create a mind map that links different emotions to their triggers and outcomes, helping you see connections and patterns.

Response Strategies:
- Pause and Plan: When you notice a strong emotion, pause and plan how to respond rather than reacting impulsively. This can prevent negative consequences and help you act in a way that aligns with your long-term goals.
- Emotion Regulation Techniques: Practice techniques such as mindfulness meditation, deep breathing, or progressive muscle relaxation to regulate your emotional responses.

Seeking Balance:
- Work-Life Balance: Ensure you have a balance between work, rest, and play to maintain emotional well-being.
- Healthy Relationships: Foster healthy relationships that support your emotional health. Recognize and address toxic relationships that contribute to emotional distress.

Benefits of Using an Emotion Compass

Improved Self-Awareness:
- Enhances understanding of your emotional states and the factors influencing them, leading to better self-awareness.

Better Decision-Making:
- Assists in making decisions that are aligned with your values and emotional well-being, reducing impulsive and regrettable choices.

Enhanced Emotional Regulation:
- Provides tools and strategies to manage emotions effectively, reducing the impact of negative emotions and enhancing positive emotional experiences.

Increased Resilience:
- Builds resilience by helping you navigate through emotional challenges with greater ease and confidence.

Healthier Relationships:
- Improves communication and understanding in relationships by fostering emotional intelligence and empathy.

An emotion compass is a valuable metaphorical tool for navigating the complex world of emotions. By fostering emotional awareness, regulation, and purposeful direction, it helps individuals achieve greater emotional balance and well-being. Regularly checking in with your emotional compass can lead to improved mental health, better decision-making, and more fulfilling relationships.

Daily Tracking

Daily mood tracking serves several purposes, depending on the individual's goals and context. Here are some common reasons why people engage in daily mood tracking:

Self-awareness and Reflection:
Tracking mood daily helps individuals become more aware of their emotions, triggers, and patterns. It allows them to reflect on what influences their mood positively or negatively.

Identifying Patterns:
By consistently tracking mood over time, patterns and trends may emerge. This can help in identifying factors such as sleep, exercise, diet, or specific activities that impact mood.

Emotional Regulation:
It can aid in developing strategies for managing emotions. When individuals track their mood daily, they can notice early signs of stress or low mood and implement coping mechanisms or self-care activities.

Goal Setting and Progress Monitoring:
Mood tracking can be part of a broader goal-setting process. For example, someone aiming to improve their overall well-being might track their mood alongside other factors like exercise frequency or meditation practice.

Communication with Healthcare Providers:
For individuals with mental health conditions, daily mood tracking can provide valuable information to healthcare providers. It gives a clearer picture of mood stability and fluctuations, which can inform treatment decisions.

Tracking Treatment Effectiveness:
If someone is undergoing therapy or taking medication, daily mood tracking helps monitor how well treatment is working. It provides data on whether interventions are helping to stabilize mood or if adjustments are needed.

Promoting Mindfulness:
The act of recording daily mood encourages mindfulness and self-reflection. It encourages individuals to check in with themselves regularly and acknowledge their emotional state.

Overall, daily mood tracking can be a powerful tool for personal growth, emotional regulation, and improving overall well-being by fostering self-awareness and informed decision-making.

Track your
Emotional state for **7** days
using the mental health
tracker.

After you have completed the
tracking, look for consistencies
in your emotional state.

Write them down.

Week 1

Focus on tracking how you operate — your thoughts, habits, emotions, and responses — to better understand your patterns and support your growth.

Mental health
Daily tracker

Date _____

Mo Tu We Th Fr Sa Su

My sleep last night was

😍 🙂 😐 😣 😫

Approx. hours _____

Get up time _____

How am I feeling this morning?

😍 Great   🙂 Good   😐 Okay   😣 Not good   😫 Awful

Day to-do list

- Brush teeth and wash face
- Open a window and get fresh air
- Get work tasks done
- Time off screens
- Eat breakfast and lunch
- Move my body or take a walk

Today I intend _____

_____

Eye exercises

1 2 3

Cups of water

1 2 3 4 5 6 7

Evening to-do list

- Read 20 pages of a book
- Write in my journal
- Meditate for 10 minutes
- Workout for 30 minutes
- Brush teeth and wash face
- Take a shower

How am I feeling this evening?

😍 Great   🙂 Good   😐 Okay   😣 Not good   😫 Awful

Am I satisfied with this day?

😍 🙂 😐 😣 😫

I am grateful today for

_____
_____
_____

What I like about myself today

_____
_____
_____

What I managed to do today

_____
_____
_____

What I would like to tell myself for tomorrow

Notes

How and what would I like to feel tomorrow

joy appreciation empowered enthusiasm fun proud
strong active love passion freedom happiness
optimism belief hope inspired courage interest
amusement gratitude delight relaxed calm confident
curious focused worthy thrilled self-respecting kind

What are eye exercises?

Eye exercises are activities or techniques designed to improve the strength, flexibility, coordination, and focusing ability of the eye muscles. These exercises are often recommended to alleviate eye strain, improve vision, and maintain overall eye health. Here are some common types of eye exercises:

1. Eye Rolling: Roll your eyes in a circular motion clockwise and then counterclockwise. This helps to loosen up the eye muscles and improve circulation around the eyes.

2. Palming: Rub your palms together vigorously until they feel warm, then place them gently over your closed eyes without applying pressure. This helps to relax the eye muscles and reduce strain.

3. Near-Far Focus: Hold your thumb about 10 inches away from your face and focus on it. Then, focus on an object farther away, such as a distant wall or a tree outside the window. Alternate between focusing near and far several times.

4. Blinking: Blink your eyes rapidly for a few seconds to moisten them and reduce dryness, which can occur when staring at screens or reading for extended periods.

5. Zooming: Hold a small object (like a pen or a finger) at arm's length and slowly bring it towards your nose, focusing on it as you move it closer. Then, slowly move it back out to arm's length while maintaining focus.

6. Figure 8s: Imagine a large figure 8 (infinity symbol) about 10 feet in front of you. Trace the figure 8 with your eyes horizontally and then vertically. This helps to improve coordination and flexibility of the eye muscles.

7. Eye Massage: Gently massage the area around your eyes using your fingertips in small circular motions. This can help relieve tension and increase blood flow to the eyes.

8. Tracking: Hold your finger or a pen at arm's length and move it slowly from side to side, up and down, or in circles while keeping your head still. Follow the object with your eyes without moving your head.

9. Focus Shifting: Place your thumb about 6 inches in front of your face and focus on it. Then, shift your focus to an object in the distance. Alternate focusing between the near and far objects.

10. Computer Screen Breaks: To prevent digital eye strain, follow the 20-20-20 rule: Every 20 minutes, look at something 20 feet away for at least 20 seconds to give your eyes a break from staring at a screen.

It's important to note that while eye exercises can be beneficial for many people, they should not replace professional eye care or treatment for serious vision problems. If you have specific concerns about your vision or experience persistent eye discomfort, consult an eye care professional for guidance tailored to your needs.

Journal It

Mental health
Daily tracker

Date _____

(Mo) (Tu) (We) (Th) (Fr) (Sa) (Su)

My sleep last night was

😍 🙂 😐 😟 😣

Approx. hours _____

Get up time _____

How am I feeling this morning?

😍 Great   🙂 Good   😐 Okay   😟 Not good   😣 Awful

Day to-do list

☐ Brush teeth and wash face   ☐ Get work tasks done   ☐ Eat breakfast and lunch   _____

☐ Open a window and get fresh air   ☐ Time off screens   ☐ Move my body or take a walk   _____

Today I intend _____

_____

Eye exercises

(1) (2) (3)

Cups of water

(1) (2) (3) (4) (5) (6) (7)

Evening to-do list

☐ Read 20 pages of a book   ☐ Meditate for 10 minutes   ☐ Brush teeth and wash face

☐ Write in my journal   ☐ Workout for 30 minutes   ☐ Take a shower

How am I feeling this evening?

😍 Great   🙂 Good   😐 Okay   😟 Not good   😣 Awful

Am I satisfied with this day?

😍 🙂 😐 😟 😣

I am grateful today for

_____

_____

_____

What I like about myself today

_____

_____

_____

What I managed to do today

_____

_____

_____

What I would like to tell myself for tomorrow

┌─────────────────────────────────────┐
│   │
│   │
│   │
└─────────────────────────────────────┘

Notes

How and what would I like to feel tomorrow

joy   appreciation   empowered   enthusiasm   fun   proud
strong   active   love   passion   freedom   happiness
optimism   belief   hope   inspired   courage   interest
amusement   gratitude   delight   relaxed   calm   confident
curious   focused   worthy   thrilled   self-respecting   kind

Why is sleep important to my mental health?

Sleep is crucial for mental health due to several interconnected reasons:

1. Restoration and Repair: During sleep, the brain undergoes essential processes that help repair and restore neurons and other cells. This is vital for maintaining optimal cognitive function, emotional regulation, and overall brain health.

2. Memory Consolidation: Sleep plays a critical role in consolidating memories, which is essential for learning and retaining information. It helps the brain process and store memories from the day, enhancing learning and problem-solving abilities.

3. Emotional Regulation: Adequate sleep is necessary for maintaining emotional stability and resilience. Sleep deprivation can lead to increased irritability, mood swings, and difficulty managing stress or emotional reactions.

4. Brain Plasticity: Sleep supports neuroplasticity, the brain's ability to reorganize itself by forming new neural connections. This is important for adapting to new experiences, learning new skills, and recovering from injuries or trauma.

5. Hormone Regulation: Sleep influences the balance of hormones that regulate stress, appetite, metabolism, and other bodily functions. Chronic sleep deprivation can disrupt these hormonal processes, contributing to mood disorders, weight gain, and other health issues.

6. Mental Health Disorders: Poor sleep is closely linked to an increased risk of developing mental health disorders such as depression, anxiety, and bipolar disorder. In individuals already experiencing these conditions, sleep disturbances can exacerbate symptoms and make recovery more challenging.

7. Cognitive Function: Sleep deprivation impairs cognitive functions such as attention, concentration, decision-making, and reaction times. This can affect daily performance at work or school and increase the risk of accidents or errors.

8. Immune Function: Sleep is also important for immune function. Chronic sleep deficiency can weaken the immune system, making individuals more susceptible to infections and illnesses.

Overall, prioritizing good sleep hygiene and ensuring an adequate amount of quality sleep each night (typically 7-9 hours for adults) is essential for promoting mental health, cognitive function, emotional well-being, and overall quality of life.

Journal It

Daily tracker

Date _____

Mo Tu We Th Fr Sa Su

My sleep last night was

😍 🙂 😕 😣 😩

Approx. hours _____

Get up time _____

How am I feeling this morning?

😍 Great   🙂 Good   😕 Okay   😣 Not good   😩 Awful

Day to-do list

☐ Brush teeth and wash face   ☐ Get work tasks done   ☐ Eat breakfast and lunch

☐ Open a window and get fresh air ☐ Time off screens   ☐ Move my body or take a walk

Today I intend _____   **Eye exercises**   **Cups of water**

_____   1 2 3   1 2 3 4 5 6 7

Evening to-do list

☐ Read 20 pages of a book   ☐ Meditate for 10 minutes   ☐ Brush teeth and wash face

☐ Write in my journal   ☐ Workout for 30 minutes   ☐ Take a shower

How am I feeling this evening?

😍 Great   🙂 Good   😕 Okay   😣 Not good   😩 Awful

Am I satisfied with this day?

😍 🙂 😕 😣 😩

I am grateful today for

_____
_____
_____

What I like about myself today

_____
_____
_____

What I managed to do today

_____
_____
_____

What I would like to tell myself for tomorrow

[   ]

Notes

How and what would I like to feel tomorrow

joy   appreciation   empowered   enthusiasm   fun   proud
strong   active   love   passion   freedom   happiness
optimism   belief   hope   inspired   courage   interest
amusement   gratitude   delight   relaxed   calm   confident
curious   focused   worthy   thrilled   self-respecting   kind

Why is water intake important to my mental health?

Water intake is crucial for mental health due to several key reasons:

1. Brain Function: The brain is made up of about 75% water. Proper hydration ensures that the brain receives enough fluid to function optimally. Water helps in the production of neurotransmitters and the maintenance of proper brain chemistry, which are essential for mood regulation, cognition, and overall mental performance.

2. Cognitive Function: Dehydration can impair cognitive abilities such as concentration, alertness, and short-term memory. Studies have shown that even mild dehydration can negatively impact cognitive function and mood.

3. Mood Regulation: Adequate hydration supports the body's ability to regulate mood. Dehydration can lead to irritability, anxiety, and changes in mood. Drinking enough water helps maintain a stable mood and promotes a sense of well-being.

4. Energy Levels: Water is essential for transporting nutrients and oxygen throughout the body, including to the brain. Proper hydration helps maintain energy levels and reduces feelings of fatigue and lethargy, which can impact mood and motivation.

5. Stress Management: When the body is dehydrated, it can increase cortisol levels, which is the hormone associated with stress. Chronic dehydration can contribute to higher stress levels and make it more difficult to cope with daily stressors.

6. Brain Structure and Function: Water plays a role in maintaining the structure of brain cells and ensuring efficient communication between neurons. It also helps regulate temperature and remove waste products from the brain, which is important for overall brain health.

7. Sleep Quality: Dehydration can interfere with sleep quality and duration. Poor sleep, in turn, can negatively impact mood, cognitive function, and overall mental health.

8. Physical Health Impact: Chronic dehydration can lead to various physical health issues such as headaches, dizziness, and fatigue, which can indirectly affect mental health by reducing overall well-being and quality of life.

In summary, staying properly hydrated by drinking an adequate amount of water each day (about 8 glasses or 2 liters for most adults) is essential for maintaining optimal mental health, cognitive function, mood regulation, and overall well-being.

Journal It

Mental health
Daily tracker

Date _____

Mo · Tu · We · Th · Fr · Sa · Su

My sleep last night was

😍 🙂 😐 😟 😞

Approx. hours _____

Get up time _____

How am I feeling this morning?

😍 Great   🙂 Good   😐 Okay   😟 Not good   😞 Awful

Day to-do list

☐ Brush teeth and wash face   ☐ Get work tasks done   ☐ Eat breakfast and lunch

☐ Open a window and get fresh air ☐ Time off screens   ☐ Move my body or take a walk

Today I intend _____

_____

Eye exercises

1 2 3

Cups of water

1 2 3 4 5 6 7

Evening to-do list

☐ Read 20 pages of a book   ☐ Meditate for 10 minutes   ☐ Brush teeth and wash face

☐ Write in my journal   ☐ Workout for 30 minutes   ☐ Take a shower

How am I feeling this evening?

😍 Great   🙂 Good   😐 Okay   😟 Not good   😞 Awful

Am I satisfied with this day?

😍 🙂 😐 😟 😞

I am grateful today for

_____
_____
_____

What I like about myself today

_____
_____
_____

What I managed to do today

_____
_____
_____

What I would like to tell myself for tomorrow

[   ]

Notes

How and what would I like to feel tomorrow

joy   appreciation   empowered   enthusiasm   fun   proud
strong   active   love   passion   freedom   happiness
optimism   belief   hope   inspired   courage   interest
amusement   gratitude   delight   relaxed   calm   confident
curious   focused   worthy   thrilled   self-respecting   kind

Why is it important to structure my day?

Structuring your day offers several important benefits for overall productivity, well-being, and mental health:

1. Time Management: Structuring your day helps you allocate time effectively to different tasks and activities. It allows you to prioritize important tasks, set realistic goals, and manage deadlines more efficiently.

2. Reduced Stress: Having a structured day can reduce feelings of overwhelm and stress. When you have a plan in place, you are less likely to feel rushed or disorganized, which can contribute to a calmer state of mind.

3. Increased Productivity: A structured day promotes productivity by creating a framework within which to accomplish tasks. It helps you stay focused and motivated, making it easier to complete tasks in a timely manner.

4. Better Focus and Concentration: When you have a clear schedule and know what needs to be done next, it becomes easier to maintain focus and concentration on the task at hand. This enhances efficiency and reduces distractions.

5. Improved Time for Self-Care: Structuring your day allows you to allocate time not only for work or responsibilities but also for self-care activities such as exercise, relaxation, hobbies, and spending time with loved ones. This balance contributes to overall well-being.

6. Consistency and Routine: A structured day establishes a daily routine, which can be comforting and reassuring. Routine provides a sense of stability and predictability, which can help reduce anxiety and improve mental health.

7. Goal Achievement: Structuring your day supports progress towards your short-term and long-term goals. By breaking down larger goals into smaller, manageable tasks and scheduling them throughout your day, you create a pathway to achievement.

8. Healthy Habits: It allows you to integrate healthy habits into your daily routine, such as regular meals, hydration, exercise, and adequate sleep. These habits are essential for maintaining physical and mental health.

9. Enhanced Time Management Skills: Practicing daily structure helps develop and improve your time management skills over time. This skill is valuable in both personal and professional contexts, contributing to long-term success and satisfaction.

Overall, structuring your day provides a framework that promotes organization, efficiency, and well-being. It helps you make the most of your time, manage stress effectively, and achieve a balanced and fulfilling lifestyle.

Journal It

Daily tracker

Date _____

Mo Tu We Th Fr Sa Su

My sleep last night was

😍 🙂 😐 🙁 😞

How am I feeling this morning?

😍 Great   🙂 Good   😐 Okay   🙁 Not good   😞 Awful

Approx. hours _____

Get up time _____

Day to-do list

- Brush teeth and wash face
- Open a window and get fresh air
- Get work tasks done
- Time off screens
- Eat breakfast and lunch
- Move my body or take a walk

Today I intend _____

_____

Eye exercises

1 2 3

Cups of water

1 2 3 4 5 6 7

Evening to-do list

- Read 20 pages of a book
- Write in my journal
- Meditate for 10 minutes
- Workout for 30 minutes
- Brush teeth and wash face
- Take a shower

How am I feeling this evening?

😍 Great   🙂 Good   😐 Okay   🙁 Not good   😞 Awful

Am I satisfied with this day?

😍 🙂 😐 🙁 😞

I am grateful today for

_____

_____

_____

What I like about myself today

_____

_____

_____

What I managed to do today

_____

_____

_____

What I would like to tell myself for tomorrow

_____

Notes

How and what would I like to feel tomorrow

joy appreciation empowered enthusiasm fun proud
strong active love passion freedom happiness
optimism belief hope inspired courage interest
amusement gratitude delight relaxed calm confident
curious focused worthy thrilled self-respecting kind

Journal It

THIS IS A
CHALLENGE THAT IS
HERE TO TEACH ME
SOMETHING

Mental health
Daily tracker

Date _____

Mo Tu We Th Fr Sa Su

My sleep last night was

😍 🙂 😐 🙁 😣

Approx. hours _____

Get up time _____

How am I feeling this morning?

😍 Great   🙂 Good   😐 Okay   🙁 Not good   😣 Awful

Day to-do list

☐ Brush teeth and wash face   ☐ Get work tasks done   ☐ Eat breakfast and lunch

☐ Open a window and get fresh air   ☐ Time off screens   ☐ Move my body or take a walk

Today I intend _____

_____

Eye exercises

1 2 3

Cups of water

1 2 3 4 5 6 7

Evening to-do list

☐ Read 20 pages of a book   ☐ Meditate for 10 minutes   ☐ Brush teeth and wash face

☐ Write in my journal   ☐ Workout for 30 minutes   ☐ Take a shower

How am I feeling this evening?

😍 Great   🙂 Good   😐 Okay   🙁 Not good   😣 Awful

Am I satisfied with this day?

😍 🙂 😐 🙁 😣

I am grateful today for

_____
_____
_____

What I like about myself today

_____
_____
_____

What I managed to do today

_____
_____
_____

What I would like to tell myself for tomorrow

```
┌─────────────────────────────────┐
│                                 │
│                                 │
│                                 │
└─────────────────────────────────┘
```

Notes

How and what would I like to feel tomorrow

joy   appreciation   empowered   enthusiasm   fun   proud
strong   active   love   passion   freedom   happiness
optimism   belief   hope   inspired   courage   interest
amusement   gratitude   delight   relaxed   calm   confident
curious   focused   worthy   thrilled   self-respecting   kind

Journal It

Mental health
Daily tracker

Date _____

Mo   Tu   We   Th   Fr   Sa   Su

My sleep last night was

😍 🙂 😐 ☹️ 😣

How am I feeling this morning?

😍 Great   🙂 Good   😐 Okay   ☹️ Not good   😣 Awful

Approx. hours _____

Get up time _____

Day to-do list

☐ Brush teeth and wash face   ☐ Get work tasks done   ☐ Eat breakfast and lunch

☐ Open a window and get fresh air   ☐ Time off screens   ☐ Move my body or take a walk

Today I intend _____

_____

Eye exercises

1   2   3

Cups of water

1   2   3   4   5   6   7

Evening to-do list

☐ Read 20 pages of a book   ☐ Meditate for 10 minutes   ☐ Brush teeth and wash face

☐ Write in my journal   ☐ Workout for 30 minutes   ☐ Take a shower

How am I feeling this evening?

😍 Great   🙂 Good   😐 Okay   ☹️ Not good   😣 Awful

Am I satisfied with this day?

😍 🙂 😐 ☹️ 😣

I am grateful today for

_____

_____

_____

What I like about myself today

_____

_____

_____

What I managed to do today

_____

_____

_____

What I would like to tell myself for tomorrow

Notes

How and what would I like to feel tomorrow

joy   appreciation   empowered   enthusiasm   fun   proud
strong   active   love   passion   freedom   happiness
optimism   belief   hope   inspired   courage   interest
amusement   gratitude   delight   relaxed   calm   confident
curious   focused   worthy   thrilled   self-respecting   kind

Journal It

"KEEP MOVING,
the best is yet to come".

Week 2

Focus on identifying your triggers, improving your mood through healthy coping tools, and setting intentional goals that support your emotional well-being.

Now What do I do?

After you have tracked your emotions and identified consistencies or patterns, there are several constructive steps you can take:

1. Reflect on Triggers and Influences:
Review your mood tracking data to identify what factors consistently influence your mood. This might include aspects like sleep patterns, diet, exercise, social interactions, work stress, or specific activities.

2. Develop Strategies for Improvement:
Once you understand the factors contributing to your mood patterns, brainstorm strategies to enhance positive moods and mitigate negative ones. For example, if you notice that lack of sleep consistently correlates with lower moods, prioritize improving your sleep hygiene.

3. Set Goals:
Use your insights to set specific goals aimed at improving your overall emotional well-being. These goals could be related to lifestyle changes, stress management techniques, or enhancing social support networks.

4. Implement Changes Gradually:
Start incorporating changes based on your findings, but do so gradually to assess their impact on your mood. It's important to give yourself time to adjust and evaluate the effectiveness of each strategy.

5. Monitor Progress:
Continue tracking your emotions to monitor how your efforts are impacting your mood over time. This helps you stay accountable and adjust strategies as needed.

6. Seek Professional Guidance if Needed:
If you find it challenging to manage your emotions or if mood patterns persist despite your efforts, consider seeking guidance from a mental health professional. They can provide personalized strategies and support tailored to your specific needs.

7. Practice Self-Compassion:
Remember to be patient with yourself throughout this process. Changing habits and managing emotions takes time and effort. Celebrate small victories and learn from setbacks along the way.

By taking these steps after identifying consistencies in your mood tracking data, you can effectively work towards improving your emotional well-being and overall quality of life.

WHAT ARE MY TRIGGERS

Over the last week you have noticed some consistent behaviors that have affected your mood. What caused the behaviors? (This will be your trigger)

☐ ....
....

☐ ....
....

☐ ....
....

☐ ....
....

☐ ....
....

☐ ....
....

☐ ....
....

☐ ....
....

☐ ....
....

☐ ....
....

☐ ....
....

☐ ....
....

☐ ....

Journal It

HOW CAN I IMPROVE MY MOOD?

What are some ways you can avoid the triggers? What are ways you can deal with the triggers?

- ☐ ....
- ☐ ....
- ☐ ....
- ☐ ....
- ☐ ....
- ☐ ....
- ☐ ....
- ☐ ....
- ☐ ....
- ☐ ....
- ☐ ....
- ☐ ....
- ☐ ....
- ☐ ....

Now....lets set some goals.

Journal It

Now let's set some

SETTING SMART GOALS

Goal 1:

Specific — What do I want to accomplish and why?

Measurable — How will I know when I have accomplished it?

Achievable — How can I accomplish this goal?

Relevant — Is this the right time for me to be working towards this goal?

Timebound — When do I want to accomplish this goal by?

Goal 2:

Specific.

Measurable.

Achievable.

Relevant.

Timebound.

Goal 3:

Specific.

Measurable.

Achievable.

Relevant.

Timebound.

Goal 4:

Specific.

Measurable.

Achievable.

Relevant.

Timebound.

SETTING SMART GOALS

Goal 1:

Specific — What do I want to accomplish and why?

Measurable — How will I know when I have accomplished it?

Achievable — How can I accomplish this goal?

Relevant — Is this the right time for me to be working towards this goal?

Timebound — When do I want to accomplish this goal by?

Goal 2:

Specific.

Measurable.

Achievable.

Relevant.

Timebound.

Goal 3:

Specific.

Measurable.

Achievable.

Relevant.

Timebound.

Goal 4:

Specific.

Measurable.

Achievable.

Relevant.

Timebound.

Journal It

Daily Changes!

Implementing daily changes can significantly empower you to respond to life's challenges with resilience and authenticity by fostering a continuous growth mindset, reinforcing positive habits, and promoting adaptability. Here's a detailed breakdown of how this works:

1. Continuous Growth Mindset

A. Embracing Learning and Improvement

- Daily Reflection

Regularly reflecting on your day helps you identify areas of improvement and acknowledge progress, fostering a mindset oriented towards growth.

- Setting Small, Achievable Goals

Implementing small, daily goals can lead to significant long-term growth, keeping you motivated and engaged in personal development.

B. Building Confidence

- Celebrating Small Wins

Recognizing and celebrating small achievements boosts self-esteem and confidence, making it easier to tackle larger challenges.

- Incremental Progress

Consistent, incremental progress in skills or habits builds a strong foundation, making it easier to handle bigger challenges with confidence.

2. Reinforcing Positive Habits

A. Establishing Routine and Discipline

Consistency

- Daily changes, such as a regular exercise routine or mindfulness practice, establish a sense of stability and control, enhancing resilience.

Habit Formation

- Positive habits, once established, require less mental energy to maintain, freeing up resources to deal with unexpected challenges effectively.

B. Enhancing Well-being

Physical Health

- Regular physical activity, balanced nutrition, and adequate sleep contribute to overall well-being, making you physically and mentally more resilient.

Mental Health

- Daily practices like meditation, journaling, or gratitude exercises improve mental health, helping you stay calm and centered in the face of adversity.

3. Promoting Adaptability

A. Flexibility and Openness to Change

Embracing Change

- Regularly making small changes in your routine encourages flexibility and reduces resistance to larger, unexpected changes.

Learning New Skills

- Continuously learning and adapting new skills enhances your ability to respond to different situations creatively and effectively.

B. Strengthening Problem-Solving Abilities

Critical Thinking

- Daily problem-solving tasks or challenges enhance your critical thinking skills, making it easier to navigate complex situations.

Resilience in Failure

- Regularly stepping out of your comfort zone and facing small failures helps you develop resilience, learning to bounce back quickly from setbacks.

4. Authenticity

A. Self-Awareness and Personal Values

Introspection

- Daily practices like journaling or meditation enhance self-awareness, helping you understand and align with your core values.

Authentic Choices

- Making intentional, value-driven choices daily ensures that your actions reflect your true self, fostering authenticity.

B. Building Genuine Relationships

Communication

- Regular, honest communication with others nurtures genuine relationships, providing a strong support system during challenging times.

Empathy and Compassion

- Daily acts of kindness and empathy build stronger connections, fostering a sense of community and mutual support.

Practical Steps for Implementing Daily Changes

1. Set Intentional Daily Goals: Start with small, achievable goals that align with your long-term aspirations.

2. Establish a Routine: Create a structured daily routine that incorporates positive habits and practices.

3. Reflect and Adjust: Regularly reflect on your progress and be open to adjusting your goals and routines as needed.

4. Celebrate Progress: Acknowledge and celebrate your daily achievements, no matter how small.

5. Seek Support: Engage with a supportive community or find an accountability partner to stay motivated.

By integrating these daily changes into your life, you cultivate a resilient and authentic approach to challenges, enabling you to navigate life's ups and downs with greater ease and confidence.

Journal It

Week 3

Focus on self-compassion — speak to yourself with kindness, honor your emotions, and give yourself grace as you grow

Words of Self-Compassion

Directions: Fill in the hearts with words of kindness, encouragement, and positivity that you can tell yourself when you are having a challenging day.

Self-compassion is beneficial for mental health for several compelling reasons. It involves treating oneself with kindness, understanding, and support in times of suffering or failure, much like one would treat a close friend. Here are the key ways in which self-compassion positively impacts mental health:

1. Reduces Negative Emotions

A. Decreasing Self-Criticism

Less Harsh Judgement
- Self-compassion helps reduce the harsh self-criticism that often accompanies mistakes or perceived inadequacies, leading to lower levels of stress, anxiety, and depression.

Balanced Perspective
- It allows for a more balanced view of oneself, acknowledging both strengths and weaknesses without undue negativity.

B. Managing Difficult Emotions

Emotional Regulation
- By practicing self-compassion, individuals become better at regulating their emotions, which can reduce the intensity and duration of negative emotional states.

Soothing and Comforting
- It provides an internal source of soothing and comfort during difficult times, reducing feelings of isolation and distress.

2. Enhances Positive Emotions

A. Promoting Self-Kindness

Increased Positive Feelings
- Self-kindness, a key component of self-compassion, fosters positive feelings towards oneself, such as love, care, and warmth.

Boosting Happiness
- Regular self-compassion practices can lead to increased levels of happiness and overall life satisfaction.

B. Encouraging Optimism

Positive Outlook
- Self-compassion encourages a more positive outlook on life and future possibilities, fostering hope and resilience.

Growth Mindset
- It supports a growth mindset, where challenges are viewed as opportunities for learning and growth rather than insurmountable obstacles.

3. Builds Resilience

A. Coping with Adversity

Adaptive Coping Strategies
- Self-compassionate individuals are more likely to use adaptive coping strategies, such as problem-solving and seeking support, rather than maladaptive ones like avoidance or rumination.

Bounce Back from Setbacks
- It helps individuals bounce back more quickly from setbacks and failures, as they are less likely to be overwhelmed by self-doubt or self-blame.

B. Enhancing Self-Efficacy
Empowerment
- By fostering a kind and supportive inner dialogue, self-compassion enhances self-efficacy and the belief in one.s ability to overcome challenges.

Motivation and Persistence
- It promotes intrinsic motivation and persistence, encouraging individuals to keep striving towards their goals even in the face of difficulties.

4. Improves Relationships

A. Reducing Social Anxiety

Less Fear of Judgment
- Self-compassion reduces the fear of negative judgment from others, which can decrease social anxiety and increase social connectedness.

More Authentic Interactions
- It encourages more authentic and vulnerable interactions with others, as individuals feel more secure in their self-worth.

B. Enhancing Empathy and Compassion for Others

Empathetic Responses
- Practicing self-compassion can increase empathy and compassion for others, fostering stronger and more supportive relationships.

Mutual Support
- It helps create a reciprocal dynamic of support and understanding in relationships, enhancing overall relational well-being.

Practical Tips for Cultivating Self-Compassion

1. Mindfulness Practice: Engage in mindfulness meditation to develop greater awareness and acceptance of your thoughts and feelings without judgment.
2. Self-Compassion Exercises: Practice exercises such as the self-compassion break, where you remind yourself of common humanity, mindfulness, and self-kindness during difficult moments.
3. Positive Self-Talk: Replace negative self-talk with encouraging and compassionate language.
4. Self-Care Routine: Develop a self-care routine that includes activities that nourish your body, mind, and spirit.
5. Seek Support: Engage in therapy or join support groups focused on self-compassion and mental health.

By integrating self-compassion into your daily life, you can significantly enhance your mental health, fostering a more resilient, positive, and connected way of living.

Practicing self-compassion involves treating yourself with kindness and understanding, particularly during times of struggle or failure. Here are several practical examples of self-compassion:

<u>Self-Kindness in Difficult Times</u>
A. Offering Gentle Support
- Self-Soothing Statements: When you make a mistake, instead of criticizing yourself, say something like, "It's okay to make mistakes; everyone does. I'll learn from this."
- Self-Hug: Physically giving yourself a hug or placing your hand over your heart can provide immediate comfort and reassurance.

B. Practicing Self-Care
- Rest and Relaxation: Allow yourself to rest when you're tired or feeling unwell, rather than pushing through exhaustion.
- Healthy Treats: Enjoy a favorite healthy treat or activity that brings you joy and comfort, such as reading a book, taking a bath, or walking in nature.

<u>Mindfulness and Emotional Awareness</u>
A. Being Present with Your Emotions
- Acknowledging Feelings: Instead of ignoring or suppressing your emotions, acknowledge them with statements like, "I am feeling really sad right now, and that's okay."
- Mindfulness Meditation: Practice mindfulness meditation to observe your thoughts and feelings without judgment, allowing you to process emotions more effectively.

B. Balanced Perspective
- Common Humanity: Remind yourself that suffering and mistakes are part of the human experience. For example, "It's normal to feel this way; others go through similar struggles too."

<u>Encouraging Positive Self-Talk</u>
A. Replacing Negative Thoughts
- Reframe Self-Criticism: If you catch yourself thinking, "I'm such a failure," reframe it to, "I'm doing my best, and it's okay to have setbacks."
- Affirmations: Use positive affirmations like, "I am worthy of love and respect," or "I have the strength to overcome challenges."

B. Celebrating Small Wins
- Acknowledge Achievements: Celebrate small accomplishments throughout your day, such as completing a task, handling a difficult situation, or simply taking care of yourself.

Setting Healthy Boundaries

A. Saying No When Necessary

- Protecting Your Time and Energy: Learn to say no to requests or obligations that overwhelm you, recognizing that it's okay to prioritize your own well-being.
- Communicating Needs: Express your needs and limits to others kindly but firmly, ensuring you respect your own boundaries.

Seeking and Accepting Support

A. Reaching Out

- Talking to a Friend: Share your feelings and struggles with a trusted friend or family member who can offer support and understanding.
- Professional Help: Seek help from a therapist or counselor if you're facing significant challenges or need professional guidance.

B. Joining Support Groups

- Community Connection: Participate in support groups or communities that focus on self-compassion and mental health, providing a sense of belonging and shared experience.

Engaging in Self-Compassionate Activities

A. Creative Expression

- Journaling: Write about your experiences, feelings, and thoughts in a compassionate manner, focusing on understanding and growth rather than judgment.
- Art and Music: Engage in creative activities like drawing, painting, or playing music, which can be therapeutic and a form of self-expression.

B. Physical Well-Being

- Exercise: Engage in physical activities that you enjoy and that make you feel good, such as yoga, dancing, or hiking.
- Healthy Eating: Nourish your body with healthy foods that you enjoy, paying attention to how they make you feel.

Practicing Gratitude and Forgiveness

A. Gratitude Exercises

- Daily Gratitude Journal: Write down things you are grateful for each day, focusing on positive aspects of your life and experiences.
- Gratitude Letters: Write letters of gratitude to yourself or others, expressing appreciation and recognizing positive contributions.

B. Forgiving Yourself

- Letting Go of Past Mistakes: Practice forgiving yourself for past mistakes or perceived failures, understanding that everyone makes errors and that they are opportunities for growth.
- Self-Compassion Mantra: Use a mantra like, "I forgive myself for not being perfect. I am enough just as I am."

By incorporating these examples of self-compassion into your daily life, you can cultivate a kinder, more supportive relationship with yourself, enhancing your overall mental well-being.

Journal It

Week 4

Be intentional about your self-care —
choose practices that nourish your mind,
body, and spirit, and make them a regular
part of your routine.

Self care is not a luxury.

It's a necessity.

SELF-CARE PLANNER

DATE:_____   S   M   T   W   T   F   S

THINGS THAT MADE ME HAPPY TODAY

- _____
- _____
- _____

SELF-CARE ACTIVITIES

- _____
- _____
- _____
- _____

WATER INTAKE

◊◊◊◊   ◊◊◊◊   ◊◊
       1 L   2 L   3 L

TODAY'S MOOD

☺ ☹ ☺ ☹ ☹ ☺ ☺

DAILY NUTRITION

Breakfast _____

Lunch _____

Dinner _____

Snacks _____

HABITS TO START

- _____
- _____
- _____
- _____

HABITS TO STOP

- _____
- _____
- _____
- _____

(Daily)
SELF-CARE

DATE ____ / ____ / ____

S M T W T F S

CHECKLIST

- ○ MAKE YOUR BED
- ○ TAKE YOUR MEDICATIONS & VITAMINS
- ○ SKINCARE ROUTINE
- ○ HEALTHY MEALS
- ○ GO FOR A WALK
- ○ CLEANING HOUSE
- ○ WASHING CLOTHES
- ○ LISTEN TO MUSIC
- ○ HAVE A POWER NAP
- ○ SOCIAL MEDIA BREAK

- ○ TAKE A LONG BATH
- ○ DO A FACE MASK
- ○ CALL A FRIEND OR FAMILY
- ○ MEDITATION
- ○ WATCH A MOVIE
- ○ CUDDLE A PET OR HUMAN
- ○ TRY A NEW RESTAURANT
- ○ MAKE TIME TO READ
- ○ TRY A NEW RECIPE
- ○ NO PHONE 30 MINS BEFORE BED

WORKOUT

- ○ CARDIO
- ○ WEIGHT
- ○ YOGA
- ○ STRETCH
- ○ REST DAY
- ○ OTHER

HOURS OF SLEEP   (Hours)

🌙 🌙 🌙 🌙 🌙 🌙 🌙 🌙
1 2 3 4 5 6 7 8

WATER BALANCE   (Glass)

1 2 3 4 5 6 7 8

THINGS THAT MAKE ME HAPPY TODAY

Action Creates Change

MOOD

ANGRY TIRED SAD GREAT FUN

5 Day Self Care Challenge

Day 1: Have Dinner with a Friend

Day 2: Go to the Beach or Park

Day 3: Have a at-home Spa Day

Day 4: Declutter your Space

Day 5: Have your Favorite Meal for Dinner

ONE WEEK SELF-CARE
CHALLENGE

Practice gratitude

Avoid social media

Have a spa day

Spend time in nature

Meditate

Make a delicious meal for yourself

Watch the sunrise

SELF-CARE DAY

TRY SIMPLE YOGA POSES

READ A NEW FUN BOOK

EAT MORE HEALTHY FOOD

DO A QUICK WORKOUT

TURN OFF SOCIAL MEDIA APP

QUICK WALK WITH PET

HAVE A PICNIC OUTSIDE

16-DAY SELF-CARE

MAKE A GRATITUDE LIST

MAKE A NEW ROUTINE

DO CREATIVE ACTIVITY

WRITE A MOOD JOURNAL

CLEAN YOUR ROOM

MAKE NEW FRIENDS

WALK IN THE NATURE

EXAMINE YOUR ROUTINE

30-Day Self Care Challenge

Take a 10-minute mindful walk	Write down 3 things you are grateful for	Cook a healthy meal for yourself	Spend 20 minutes meditating	Write a letter to your future self
Practice deep breathing for 10 minutes	Call or meet a friend for a heart-to-heart talk	Take a break from your mobile phone for the entire day	Try a new yoga pose	Take a long, relaxing bath
Visit a park or natural reserve	Listen to your favorite music	Spend time with a pet	Do a random act of kindness	Say "No" to a commitment you're not excited about
Write about a happy memory	Try a new hobby or revisit an old one	Watch your favorite movie	Go to bed half an hour earlier	Do something spontaneous
Buy yourself a small gift	Read a chapter of a book	Try a new tea or coffee flavor	Spend time in the sun	Write down 3 things you love about yourself
Practice mindfulness while doing a daily task	Take the day off chores and errands	Practice self-massage	Do something creative	Reflect on the progress you've made this month

30-DAY SELF-CARE CHALLENGE

- [ ] Set a personal goal for the month
- [ ] Practice deep breathing or meditation for 10 minutes
- [ ] Write a list of 10 things you're grateful for
- [ ] Take a walk outside
- [ ] Declutter a room or workspace

- [ ] Call or text a friend to catch up
- [ ] Cook a healthy meal
- [ ] Practice yoga or gentle stretching
- [ ] Write a positive affirmation and repeat it throughout the day
- [ ] Create a relaxing bedtime routine

- [ ] Journal about your thoughts and feelings
- [ ] Set aside time for your favorite hobby
- [ ] Give yourself a compliment
- [ ] Unplug from technology for an hour
- [ ] Listen to your favorite music or a calming playlist

- [ ] Practice mindfulness while doing everyday tasks
- [ ] Spend time with a pet or visit a local animal shelter
- [ ] Read a book or watch a movie that inspires you
- [ ] Explore a new relaxation method, like progressive muscle relaxation
- [ ] Take a power nap or restorative break

- [ ] Create a vision board or list of personal goals
- [ ] Volunteer or perform a random act of kindness
- [ ] Treat yourself to a small indulgence
- [ ] Reflect on your accomplishments and growth
- [ ] Connect with nature by visiting a park, beach, or forest

- [ ] Write a letter to your future self
- [ ] Set boundaries to protect your energy and time
- [ ] Establish a morning routine that energizes you
- [ ] Practice self-compassion and forgive yourself for past mistakes
- [ ] Review your progress and celebrate your achievements

Journal It

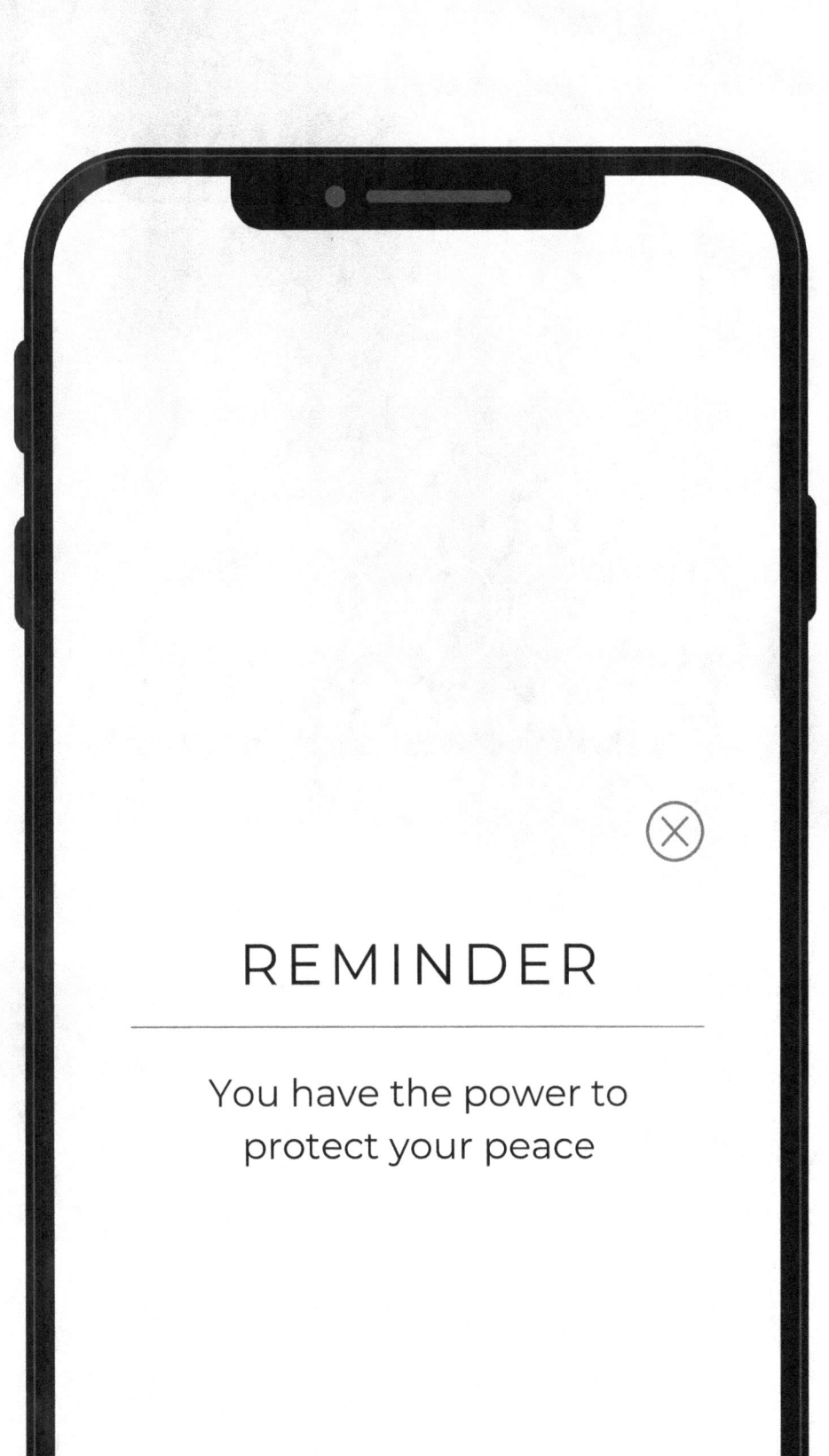

REMINDER

You have the power to
protect your peace

Appendix

All of the documents featured in this book are available for free at our Etsy shop:
Authentikxpressions —

https://authentikxpressions.etsy.com

Daily tracker

Date _____

Mo · Tu · We · Th · Fr · Sa · Su

My sleep last night was

😍 🙂 😐 😟 😢

How am I feeling this morning?

😍 Great   🙂 Good   😐 Okay   😟 Not good   😢 Awful

Approx. hours _____

Get up time _____

Day to-do list

- Brush teeth and wash face
- Open a window and get fresh air
- Get work tasks done
- Time off screens
- Eat breakfast and lunch
- Move my body or take a walk

Today I intend _____

_____

Eye exercises

1 2 3

Cups of water

1 2 3 4 5 6 7

Evening to-do list

- Read 20 pages of a book
- Write in my journal
- Meditate for 10 minutes
- Workout for 30 minutes
- Brush teeth and wash face
- Take a shower

How am I feeling this evening?

😍 Great   🙂 Good   😐 Okay   😟 Not good   😢 Awful

Am I satisfied with this day?

😍 🙂 😐 😟 😢

I am grateful today for

_____
_____
_____

What I like about myself today

_____
_____
_____

What I managed to do today

_____
_____
_____

What I would like to tell myself for tomorrow

Notes

How and what would I like to feel tomorrow

joy   appreciation   empowered   enthusiasm   fun   proud
strong   active   love   passion   freedom   happiness
optimism   belief   hope   inspired   courage   interest
amusement   gratitude   delight   relaxed   calm   confident
curious   focused   worthy   thrilled   self-respecting   kind

WHAT ARE MY TRIGGERS

Over the last week you have noticed some consistent behaviors that have affected your mood. What caused the behaviors? (This will be your trigger)

- [ ] ....
- [ ] ....
- [ ] ....
- [ ] ....
- [ ] ....
- [ ] ....
- [ ] ....
- [ ] ....
- [ ] ....
- [ ] ....
- [ ] ....
- [ ] ....
- [ ] ....
- [ ] ....

HOW CAN I IMPROVE MY MOOD?

What are some ways you can avoid the triggers? What are ways you can deal with the triggers?

☐ ....

☐ ....

☐ ....

☐ ....

☐ ....

☐ ....

☐ ....

☐ ....

☐ ....

☐ ....

☐ ....

☐ ....

☐ ....

Now.....lets set some goals.

SETTING SMART GOALS

Goal 1:

Specific — What do I want to accomplish and why?
....
Measurable — How will I know when I have accomplished it?
....
Achievable — How can I accomplish this goal?
....
Relevant — Is this the right time for me to be working towards this goal?
....
Timebound — When do I want to accomplish this goal by?
....

Goal 2:

Specific.
....
Measurable.
....
Achievable.
....
Relevant.
....
Timebound.
....

Goal 3:

Specific.
....
Measurable.
....
Achievable.
....
Relevant.
....
Timebound.
....

Goal 4:

Specific.
....
Measurable.
....
Achievable.
....
Relevant.
....
Timebound.
....

WHEEL OF
LIFE

THE WHEEL OF LIFE IS A GREAT TOOL THAT HELPS YOU BETTER UNDERSTAND WHAT YOU CAN DO TO MAKE YOUR LIFE MORE BALANCED. THINK ABOUT THE 8 LIFE CATEGORIES BELOW, AND RATE THEM FROM 1 - 10.

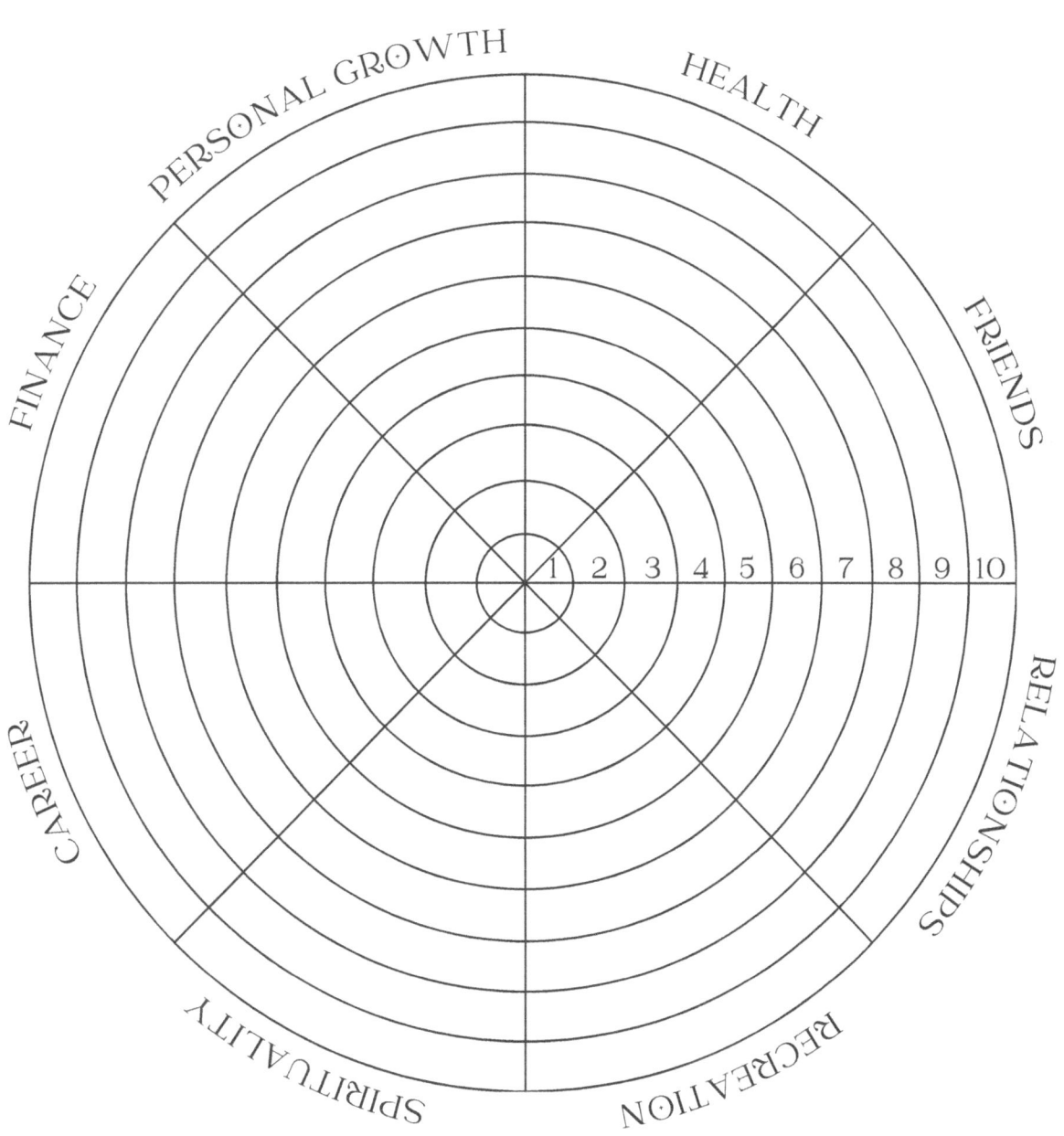

SETTING SMART GOALS

Goal 1:

Specific — What do I want to accomplish and why?

Measurable — How will I know when I have accomplished it?

Achievable — How can I accomplish this goal?

Relevant — Is this the right time for me to be working towards this goal?

Timebound — When do I want to accomplish this goal by?

Goal 2:

Specific.

Measurable.

Achievable.

Relevant.

Timebound.

Goal 3:

Specific.

Measurable.

Achievable.

Relevant.

Timebound.

Goal 4:

Specific.

Measurable.

Achievable.

Relevant.

Timebound.

- SELF-CARE DAY
- TRY SIMPLE YOGA POSES
- READ A NEW FUN BOOK
- EAT MORE HEALTHY FOOD
- DO A QUICK WORKOUT
- TURN OFF SOCIAL MEDIA APP
- QUICK WALK WITH PET
- HAVE A PICNIC OUTSIDE

16-DAY SELF-CARE

- MAKE A GRATITUDE LIST
- MAKE A NEW ROUTINE
- DO CREATIVE ACTIVITY
- WRITE A MOOD JOURNAL
- CLEAN YOUR ROOM
- MAKE NEW FRIENDS
- WALK IN THE NATURE
- EXAMINE YOUR ROUTINE

30-Day Self Care Challenge

Take a 10-minute mindful walk	Write down 3 things you are grateful for	Cook a healthy meal for yourself	Spend 20 minutes meditating	Write a letter to your future self
Practice deep breathing for 10 minutes	Call or meet a friend for a heart-to-heart talk	Take a break from your mobile phone for the entire day	Try a new yoga pose	Take a long, relaxing bath
Visit a park or natural reserve	Listen to your favorite music	Spend time with a pet	Do a random act of kindness	Say "No" to a commitment you're not excited about
Write about a happy memory	Try a new hobby or revisit an old one	Watch your favorite movie	Go to bed half an hour earlier	Do something spontaneous
Buy yourself a small gift	Read a chapter of a book	Try a new tea or coffee flavor	Spend time in the sun	Write down 3 things you love about yourself
Practice mindfulness while doing a daily task	Take the day off chores and errands	Practice self-massage	Do something creative	Reflect on the progress you've made this month

30-DAY SELF-CARE CHALLENGE

☐ Set a personal goal for the month	☐ Practice deep breathing or meditation for 10 minutes	☐ Write a list of 10 things you're grateful for	☐ Take a walk outside	☐ Declutter a room or workspace
☐ Call or text a friend to catch up	☐ Cook a healthy meal	☐ Practice yoga or gentle stretching	☐ Write a positive affirmation and repeat it throughout the day	☐ Create a relaxing bedtime routine
☐ Journal about your thoughts and feelings	☐ Set aside time for your favorite hobby	☐ Give yourself a compliment	☐ Unplug from technology for an hour	☐ Listen to your favorite music or a calming playlist
☐ Practice mindfulness while doing everyday tasks	☐ Spend time with a pet or visit a local animal shelter	☐ Read a book or watch a movie that inspires you	☐ Explore a new relaxation method, like progressive muscle relaxation	☐ Take a power nap or restorative break
☐ Create a vision board or list of personal goals	☐ Volunteer or perform a random act of kindness	☐ Treat yourself to a small indulgence	☐ Reflect on your accomplishments and growth	☐ Connect with nature by visiting a park, beach, or forest
☐ Write a letter to your future self	☐ Set boundaries to protect your energy and time	☐ Establish a morning routine that energizes you	☐ Practice self-compassion and forgive yourself for past mistakes	☐ Review your progress and celebrate your achievements

(Daily)
SELF-CARE

DATE ___ / ___ / ___

S M T W T F S

CHECKLIST

- ◯ MAKE YOUR BED
- ◯ TAKE YOUR MEDICATIONS & VITAMINS
- ◯ SKINCARE ROUTINE
- ◯ HEALTHY MEALS
- ◯ GO FOR A WALK
- ◯ CLEANING HOUSE
- ◯ WASHING CLOTHES
- ◯ LISTEN TO MUSIC
- ◯ HAVE A POWER NAP
- ◯ SOCIAL MEDIA BREAK

- ◯ TAKE A LONG BATH
- ◯ DO A FACE MASK
- ◯ CALL A FRIEND OR FAMILY
- ◯ MEDITATION
- ◯ WATCH A MOVIE
- ◯ CUDDLE A PET OR HUMAN
- ◯ TRY A NEW RESTAURANT
- ◯ MAKE TIME TO READ
- ◯ TRY A NEW RECIPE
- ◯ NO PHONE 30 MINS BEFORE BED

WORKOUT

- ◯ CARDIO
- ◯ WEIGHT
- ◯ YOGA
- ◯ STRETCH
- ◯ REST DAY
- ◯ OTHER

HOURS OF SLEEP   (Hours)

☾ ☾ ☾ ☾ ☾ ☾ ☾ ☾
1 2 3 4 5 6 7 8

WATER BALANCE   (Glass)

1 2 3 4 5 6 7 8

THINGS THAT MAKE ME HAPPY TODAY

Action Creates Change

MOOD

☹ 😐 🙁 🙂 😄
ANGRY TIRED SAD GREAT FUN

Coping Skills
and
Active
Grounding
Techniques

COPING

Now that you have come to be in your present moment and are grounded most of your overwhelming feelings have dissipated or decreased. This is the time you use coping skills. Coping skills are things we all do to distract ourselves from things. We do this daily. Our bodies automatically do things to protect us from various emotions on a daily basis. You may use coping skills and not even realize it.

Coping skills can be anything that helps you to move on from something negative and distracts you from those emotions. It could be journalling, taking a walk, taking a shower, listening to music, watching television, watching your favorite episode of something, or playing a video game. Coping skills help you to better deal with the situation however, because you have grounded yourself already the coping skills you use will be more effective.

Now try a coping skill:

- PositiveSelf-Talk
- Self-talk is engaging in thoughts that will encourage you in making it through the anxious times you experience.
- Read שׁ Repeat positive affirmations
- Aromatherapy (smell something pleasant and inhale deeply)
- Deep breathing

COPING SKILLS

Exercise.

Put on fake tattoos.

Write (poetry, stories, journal).

Scribble/doodle on paper.

Be with other people.

Watch a favorite TV show.

Hydrate.

Go see a movie.

Do a wordsearch or crossword.

Do schoolwork.

Play a musical instrument.

Paint your nails, do your make-up or hair.

Sing.

Study the sky.

Punch a pillow.

Cover yourself with Band-Aids where you want to cut.

Let yourself cry.

Take a nap (only if you are tired).

Take a hot shower or relaxing bath.

Play with a pet.

Go shopping.

Clean something.

Knit or sew.

Read a good book.

Listen to music.

Try some aromatherapy (candle, lotion, room spray).

Meditate.

Go somewhere very public.

Bake cookies.

Create a vision board.

Paint or draw.

Rip paper into itty-bitty pieces.

Shoot hoops, kick a ball.

Write a letter or send an email.

Plan your dream room (colors/furniture).

Hug a pillow or stuffed animal.

Hyperfocus on something like a rock, hand, etc.

Dance.

Make hot chocolate, a milkshake or a smoothie.

Play with modeling clay or Play-Doh.

Build a pillow fort.

Go for a nice, long drive.

Complete something you've been putting off.

Draw on yourself with a marker.

Take up a new hobby.

Look up recipes, cook a meal.

Go outside for 15 minutes.

Create or build something.

Pray.

Make a list of blessings in your life.

Read the Bible.

Go to a friend's house.

Jump on a trampoline.

Watch an old, happy movie.

Contact a hotline/your therapist, if you want, you can call us 988.

Talk to someone close to you.

Ride a bicycle.

Feed the ducks, birds, or squirrels.

Color.

Memorize a poem, play, or song.

Stretch.

Look at yourlifeyourvoice.org.

COPING SKILLS

Search for ridiculous things on the internet.
„Shop" online (without buying anything).
Color-coordinate your wardrobe.
Watch fish.
Make a playlist of your favorite songs.
Play the „15 minute game." (Avoid something for 15 minutes, when time is up start again.)
Plan your wedding/prom/other event.
Plant some seeds.
Hunt for your perfect home or car online.
Try to make as many words out of your full name as possible.
Sort through/edit your pictures.
Play with a balloon.
Give yourself a facial.
Play with a favorite childhood toy.
Start collecting something.
Play video/computer games.
Clean up trash at your local park
Text or call a friend.
Write yourself an "I love you because ..." letter.
Look up new words and use them.
Rearrange furniture.
Write a letter to someone that you may never send.
Smile at five people.
Play with your little brother/sister/niece/nephew.
Go for a walk (with or without a friend).
Put a puzzle together.
Clean your room /closet.
Try to do handstands, cartwheels, or backbends.
Yoga.
Teach your pet a new trick.
Learn a new language.
Move EVERYTHING in your room to a new spot.
Get together with friends and play Frisbee, soccer or basketball.
Hug a friend or family member.
Search online for new songs/artists.
Make a list of goals for the week/month/year/5 years.
Perform a random act of kindness

Believe in
you

GET ACTIVE

(this doesn.t mean go excercise)

Being active means to get up and do something.

Move around.
Be Busy.
Being proactive.

When dealing with anxiety it is important to
<u>actively</u> do things to help decrease the unhealthy
anxiety you are experiencing. Being active and
intentional
about what you do and how you do it
is an important step to decreasing and releasing
your excess anxiety.

ACTIVE GROUNDING

Name 5 things you can see

Name 4 things you can feel

Name 3 things you can hear

Name 2 things you can smell

Name 1 thing you can taste

ACTIVE GROUNDING

PICK 3 COLORS 1 AT A TIME NAME EVERYTHING YOU SEE IN THAT COLOR NOW COLOR # 2, THEN #3

PICK 2 SHAPES 1 AT A TIME NAME EVERYTHING YOU SEE IN THAT SHAPE NOW DO THE SAME FOR SHAPE # 2

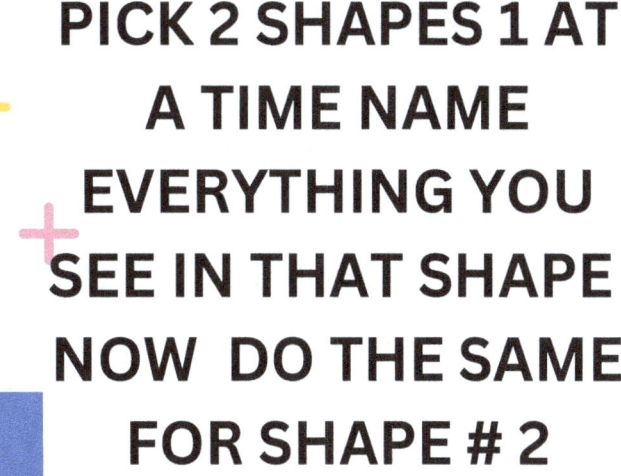

Resources

Looking for a therapist

Psychology Today

maddtherapy.com

https://authentikxpressions.etsy.com

Resources

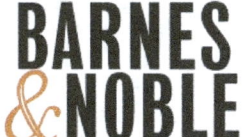